Free Flow

Fresh Air for Tough Times

Author/Illustrator
Heather Hawk Maxwell

Published by
Create Thrive Grow
Madison, Wisconsin

ISBN   978-0-99675270-1

© 2015 by Create Thrive Grow

All rights reserved. The drawings and meditations in this book are provided for personal use of the reader. No part of this book may be reproduced or transmitted in any form or by any means, electronic or mechanical, including photocopying, recording, or by any information storage and retrieval system, without written permission from the author, except by a reviewer, who may quote a brief passage in review.

The information in this book is distributed on an "as is" basis, without warranty. Every precaution has been taken in the preparation of this book to ensure that the material is factual. The author shall not have any liability to any person or entity with respect to any liability, loss, or damage caused or alleged to be caused directly or indirectly by the information contained in this book.

Create Thrive Grow
Madison, Wisconsin

CreateThriveGrow.com
joyfulhawk@att.net

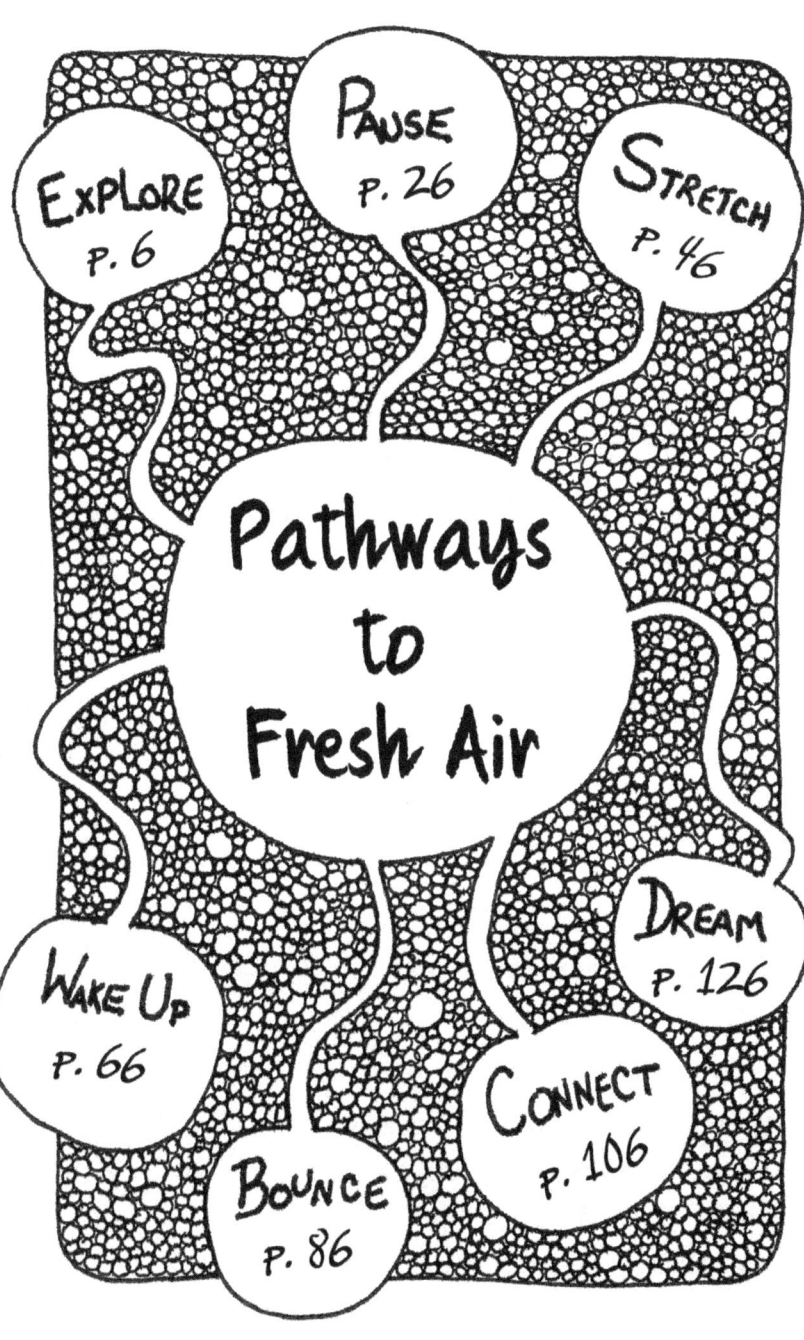

FRESH AIR

PAGES ARE PRESENTED IN PAIRS WITH THE LEFT-FACING PAGE SUGGESTING AN OBSERVATION AND THE RIGHT-FACING PAGE OFFERING A BITE-SIZED MEDITATION TO HELP BRING THE OBSERVATION TO LIFE.

Life happens one moment at a time and change happens one choice at a time. So, rather than being filled with thousands of words like most books, *Free Flow* offers a breath of fresh air. Each page contains a drawing and a few words pointing toward a single thought, chunks that we can absorb the same way that life unfolds.

FREEDOM

When stickiness is present in our lives, but unconscious, it rules us and we are powerless to change. Freedom comes from noticing.

The power of *Free Flow* lies in making it your own. Add color to the images while you listen to your thoughts. What is your reaction? Make notes or add your own drawings.

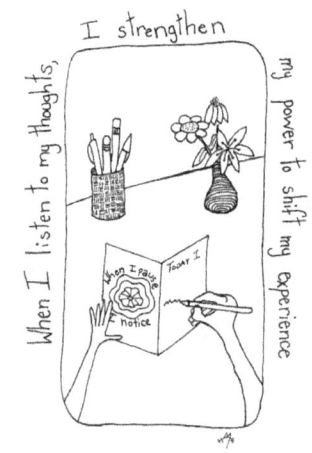

PERSONALIZE THE PAGES TO MAKE NOT ONLY THE BOOK, BUT ALSO THE IDEAS, YOUR OWN.

Today I pause and shake my body whenever I feel rigid and full of jagged edges.

Stretch

FLOW

When baby birds hatch, they are blind and without feathers. But one worm, bug, or caterpillar, and one wing flap at a time, they transform into creatures that fly through the air with grace and ease.

Like a baby bird learning to fly, with regular practice, you too can learn to experience greater flow. Each page offers an opportunity to practice. Try reading a page when you get up, before you go to bed, or during any moment you are struggling.

Practice makes perfect

SHIFT REQUIRES PRACTICE. WHEN WE WORK IN SMALL CHUNKS, WE INCREASE OUR CHANCES OF SUCCESS.

UNIVERSAL EXPERIENCES

Who has ever felt stuck? Who has ever had a hard day?

WE ALL KNOW FEELING STUCK. WE ALL KNOW BAD DAYS. WE ALL BENEFIT FROM HAVING A COMPANION TO PROVIDE FRESH AIR DURING TOUGH TIMES.

Free Flow stems from a commitment I made to myself to notice when I felt good and when I felt bad for 100 consecutive days, and to draw what I observed. Patterns emerged. I noticed that drawings I created one day helped to support me on other days. Then I noticed that my drawings applied to other people as well. When I began to share my creations, people loved how my drawings and meditations supported them. Many people asked me to gather my work together in a book. *Free Flow* is the result.

Explore

Today I approach everything, even the familiar, with fresh eyes, as if I'm seeing it for the first time. I am filled with wonder and awe.

Today, if I hit a wall I will not resist it. Instead, I will turn. Rounding the corner will open up a whole new vista of possibility.

Today I remember that even the most ordinary experiences and objects become an adventure when I observe ever-greater layers of detail.

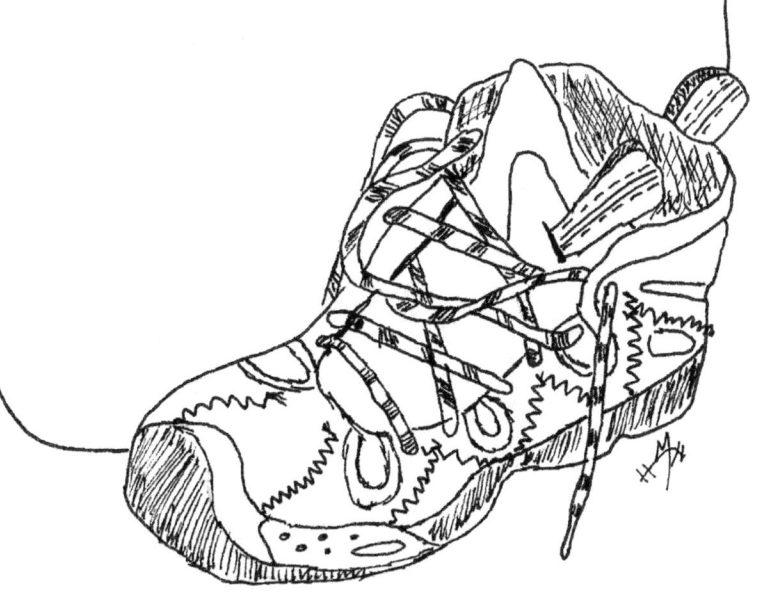

Today I remind myself that it is my job to discover the awe and wonder present in all things.

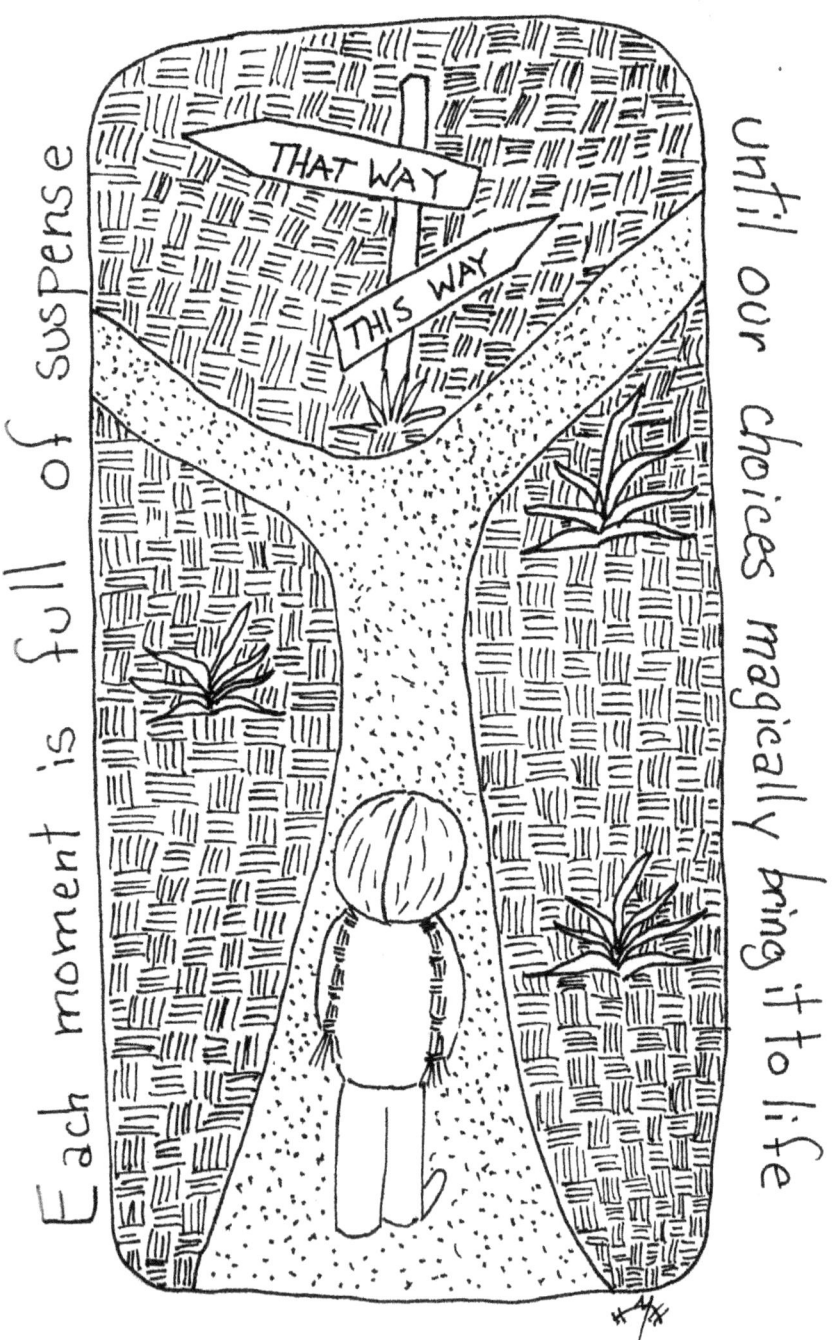

Pause

Life is sweeter by the sip

TODAY I FEEL MY CONNECTION TO THE EARTH. TODAY ALL IS WELL IN MY WORLD.

not seeing all the food that you will eat during your life all at once...

It is less overwhelming bite by bite.

There is something to be said for

Today I pause to remember what I really want and why. And then I practice allowing these to guide me through my day.

Today I practice pausing to reconnect with my calm center.

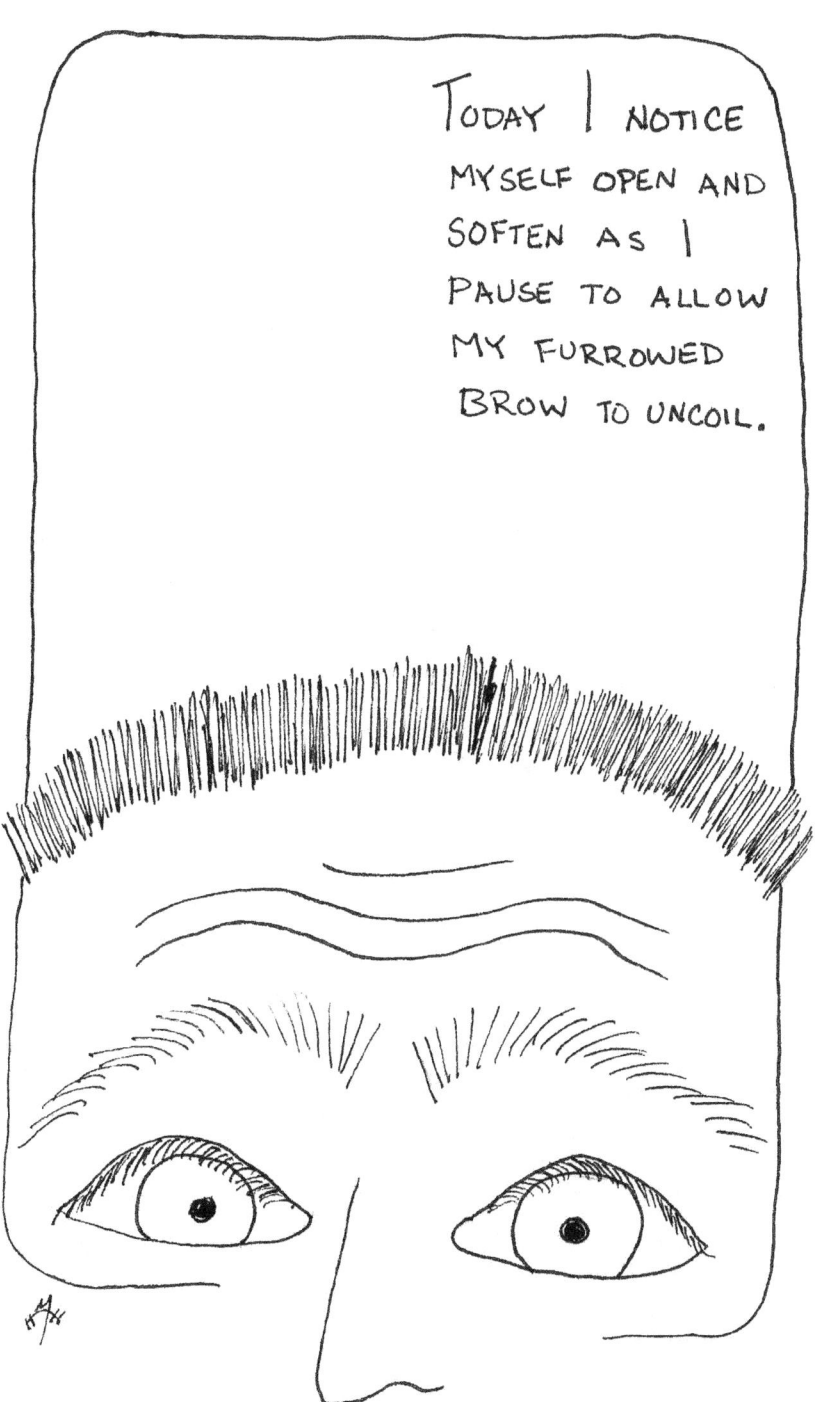

BREATHING IN
I soften
BREATHING OUT
I radiate love

I LISTEN QUIETLY, OPEN TO INSTRUCTION. TEACH ME THE MESSAGES IN MY BREATH AND THE POWER TO SHIFT MY MESSAGE BY SHIFTING MY BREATH.

the rocks in our heart,
Only when we crumble
can we grow wildflowers

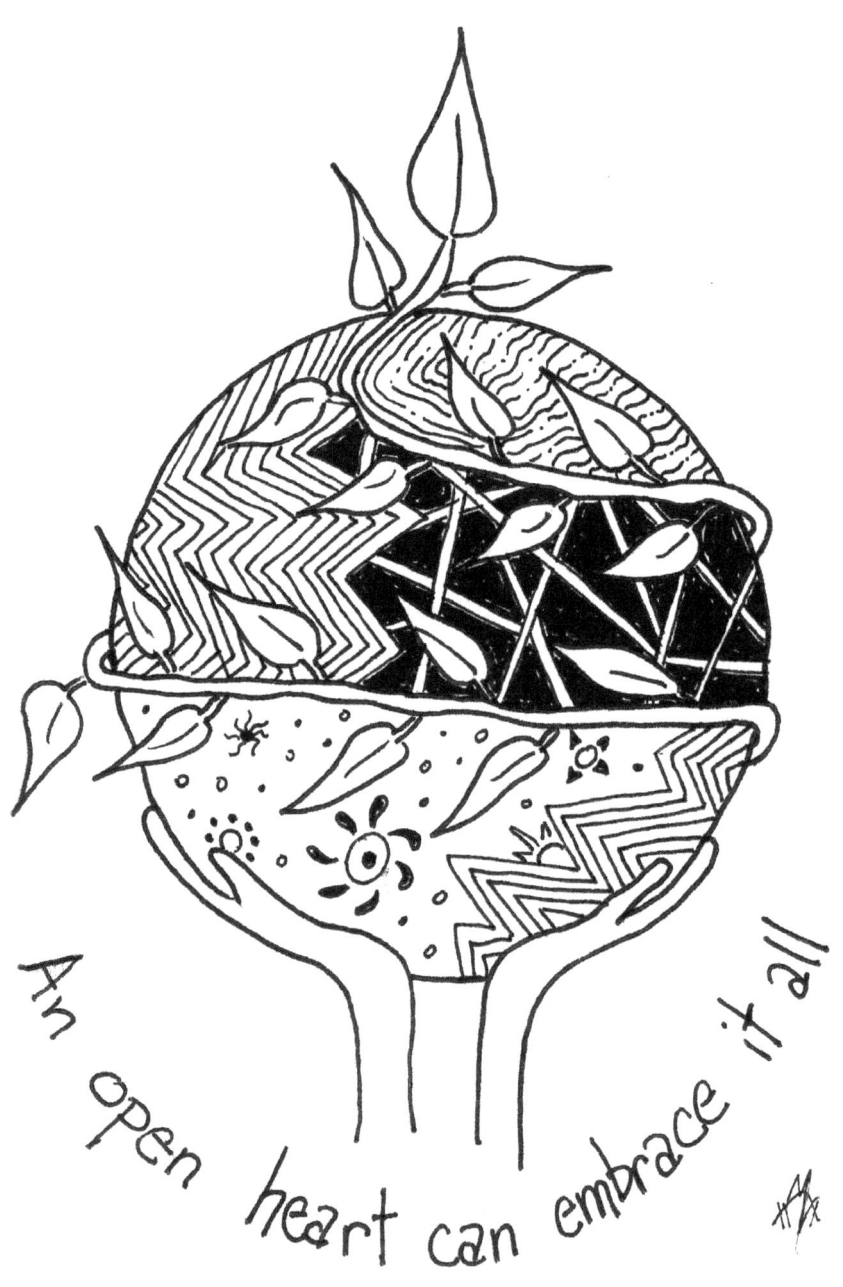

Today I feel my heart stretch wider open as I let go of anger, fear, disappointment and defensiveness.

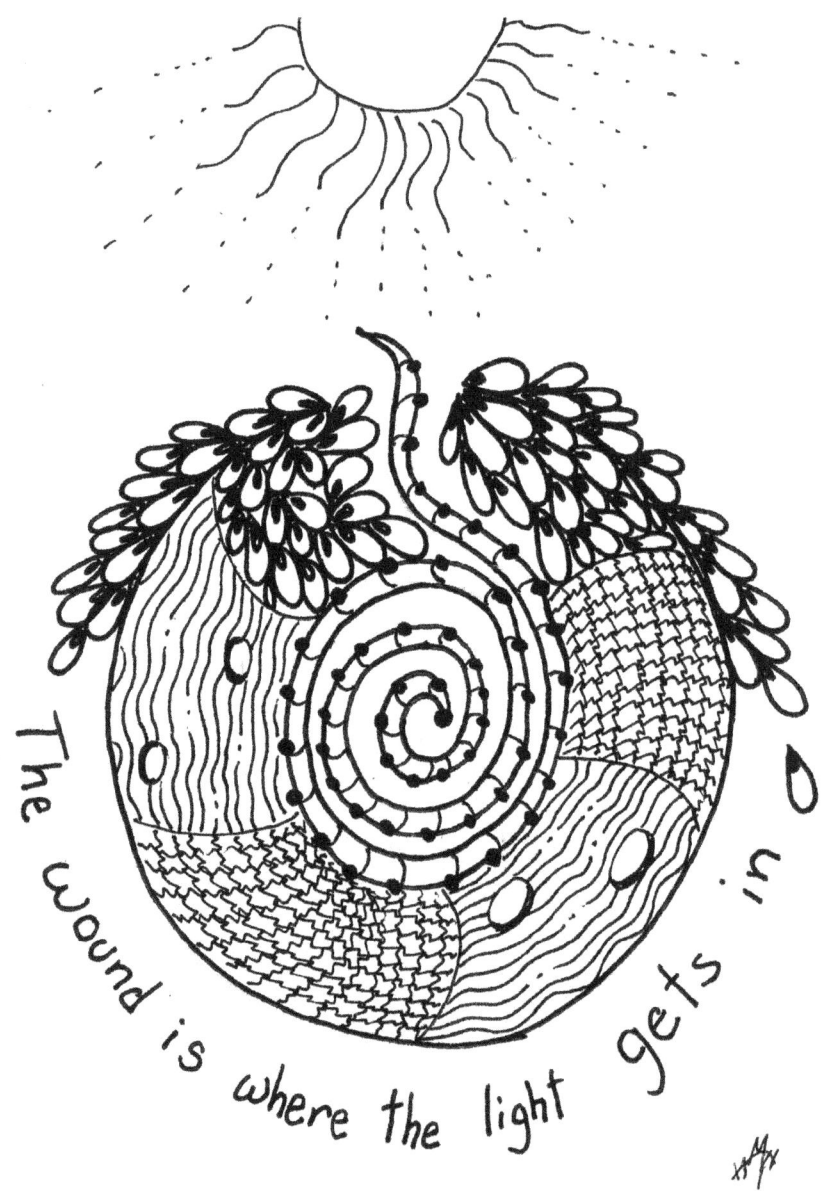

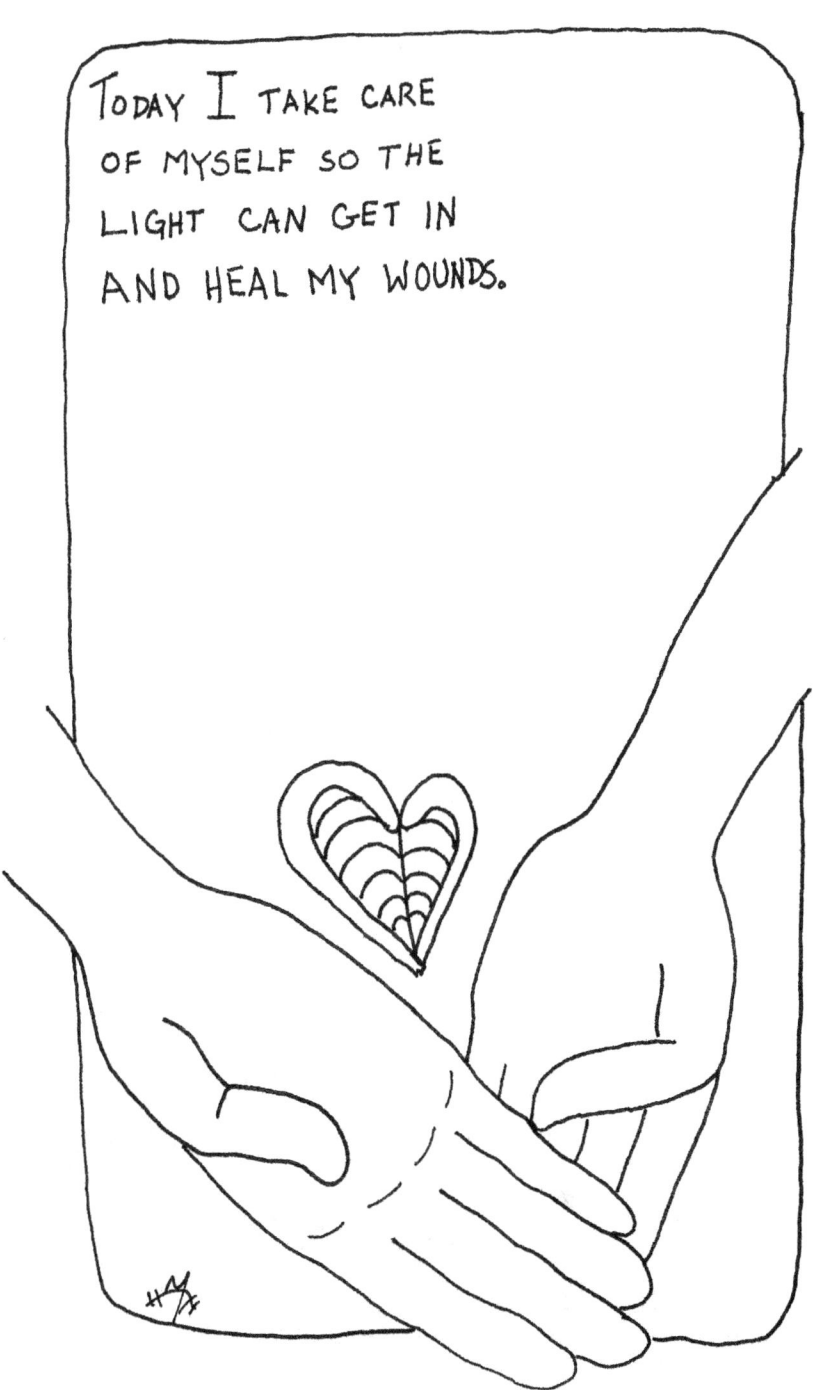

When we pause to calm our mind, our afflictions begin to dissolve

Today I remind Fear that the past does not predict the future. And I remind Fear that I am courageous, creative and persistent.

Like young hawks, we need lots of practice to learn how to use our power gracefully

Please, please, please, today may I see the crack where the light gets in. May I allow the light to open my heart and feed me.

FEARFUL SELF: Hang on for dear life!

TRUSTING SELF: You are safe. Let go.

Today may I let go and trust in soft landings.

when we view stress as an adventure rather than as an obstacle Imagine what becomes possible

Today I get through the day one breath at a time. I return to my center with each breath in and I let go with each breath out.

When we learn to embrace life's paradoxes, we are able to love in spite of pain

During my silence today, I incline my heart toward tolerance & kindness, even for those with whom I disagree.

Wake Up

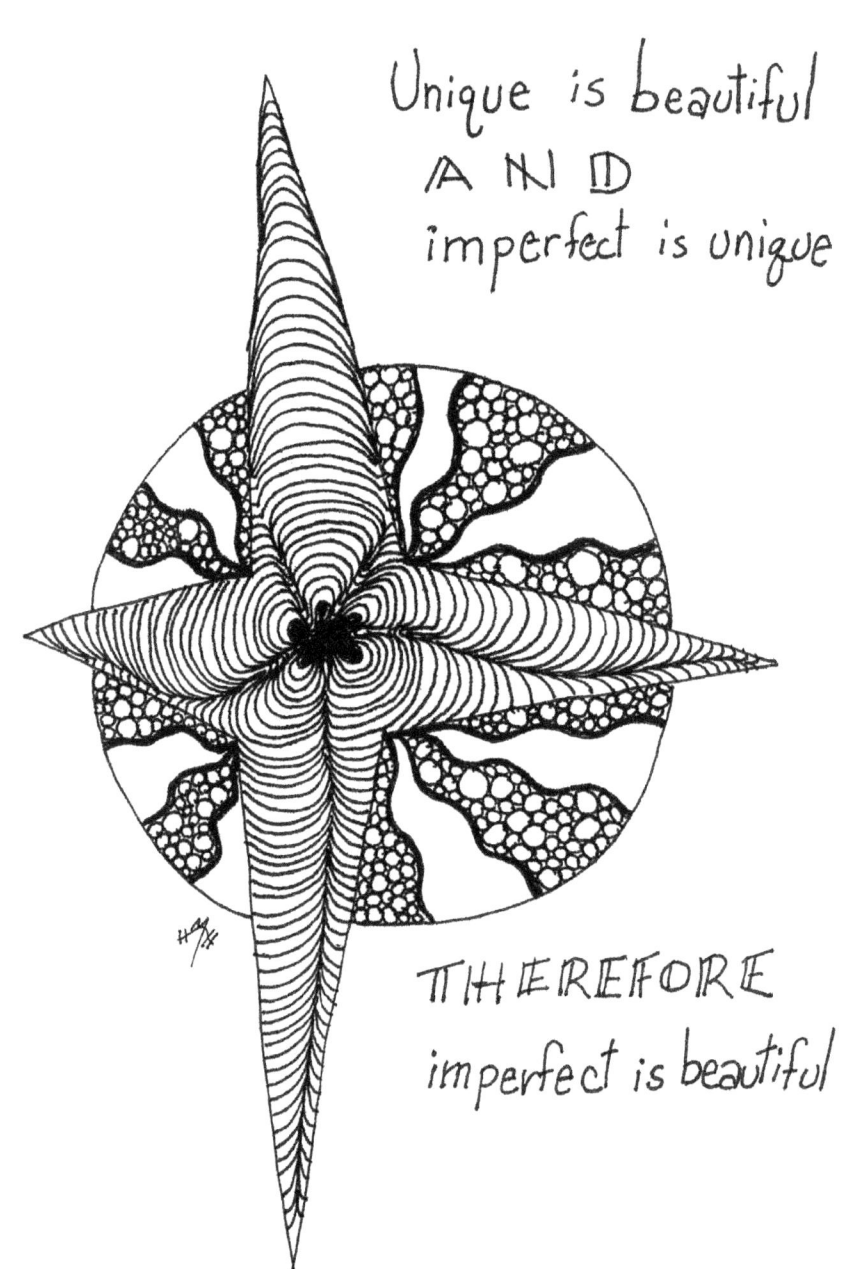

Today I remember
I am beautiful...
imperfections and all.

TODAY I SEEK OUT SOFT THINGS.

Today I am a powerful detective honing my skills to distinguish between true obstacles and simple bumps in the path.

Today I practice noticing when I contract — the subtle shifts in energy that feel like a balloon deflating.

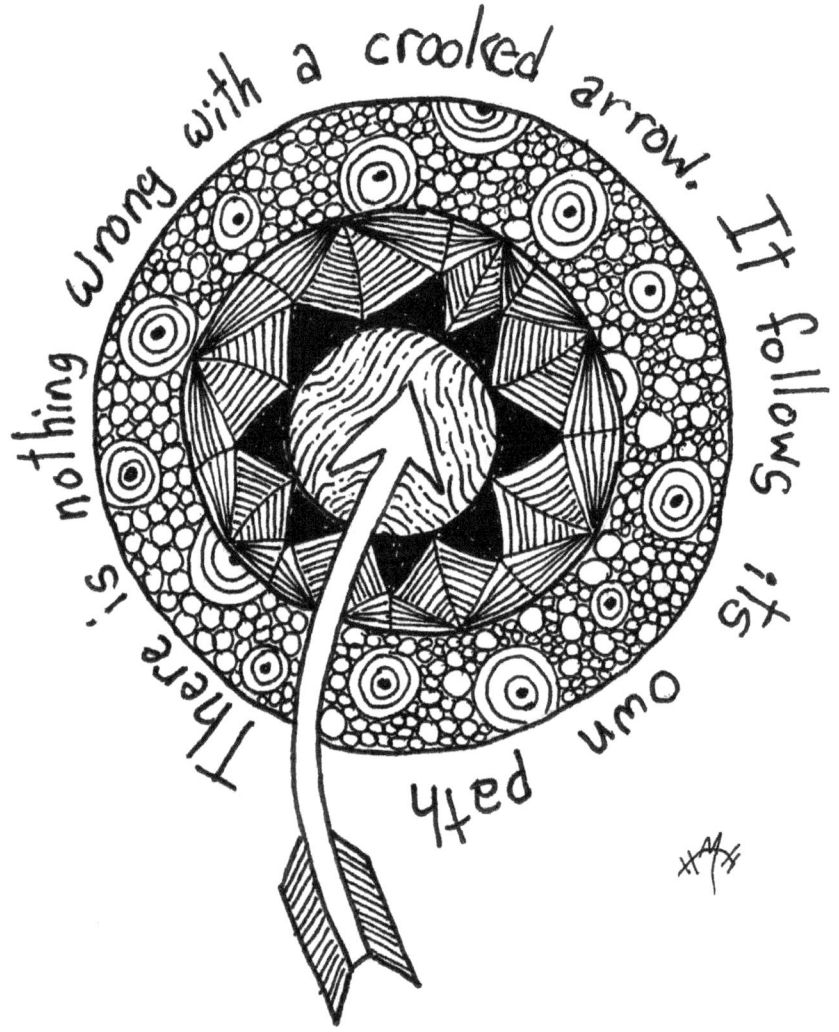

Today I remember the world is a better place because of my unique contributions.

BREATHING IN
I am proud to be me
BREATHING OUT
I am powerful

Bounce

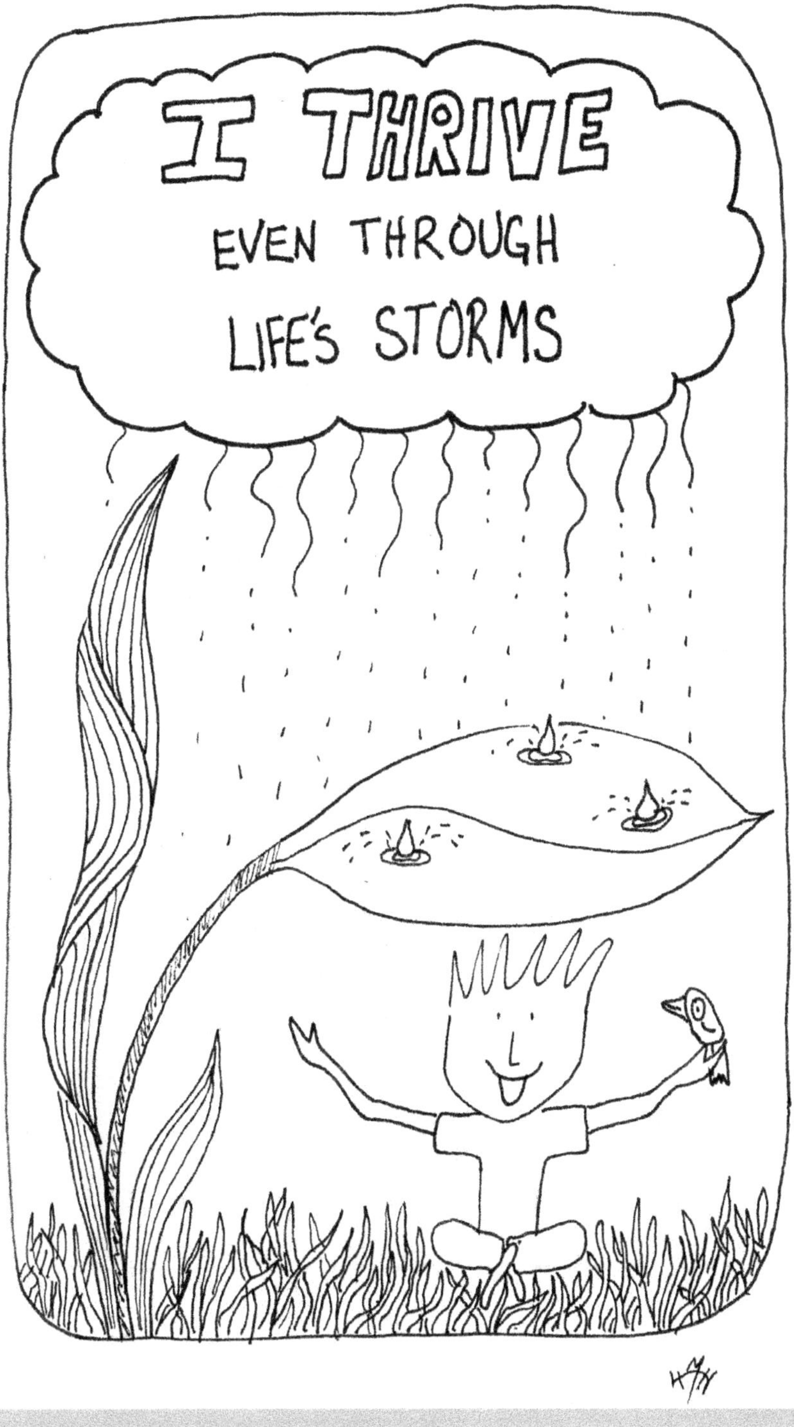
I THRIVE
EVEN THROUGH
LIFE'S STORMS

part of us believes we must brace ourselves for life's next threat

It is difficult to TRUST and RELAX when

When we are convinced it is impossible to add another ball, sometimes the Universe does it anyway

Today I practice saying 'no' and throwing back extra balls.

Today I practice focusing on flow. I allow obstacles to guide me rather than stop me.

When we embrace risk and the unknown fear cannot take root

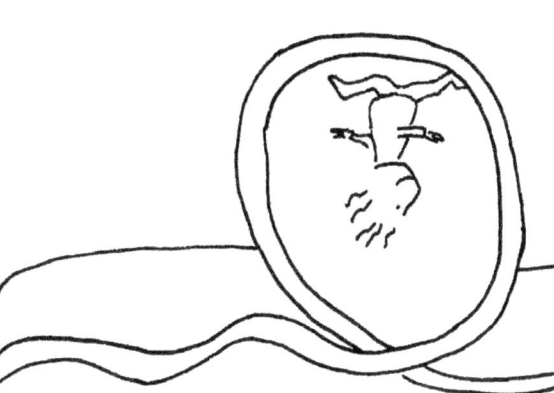

Today I remember life's twists, turns & bumps are the natural order of things. They are an integral part of my path, and a component of my ultimate success.

TODAY I PRACTICE ACCESSING MY CALM CENTER SO THAT I KNOW THE PATH TO IT WELL AND CAN FIND MY WAY THERE EVEN WHEN STORMS RAGE AROUND ME.

I BREATHE IN
POWER
I BREATHE OUT
PEACE

TODAY I AM RESILIENT.
I READILY RETURN
TO EQUILIBRIUM
WHEN I TIP.

Today I remember to take breaks to rest in order to keep up my strength for portaging life's canoes.

Connect

As I move through this day
may I raise my arms
around others facing difficulties.
And may I seek out people
to surround me as
I endure my own tough moments.

Today I see myself in others as they love, grieve, and dream. May I support, comfort and encourage them in the same way I hope others would do for me.

The same qualities that make us special have the power to make us feel like we don't fit in

Today may I remember the people I really want to be around are the people who love me precisely because I am me.

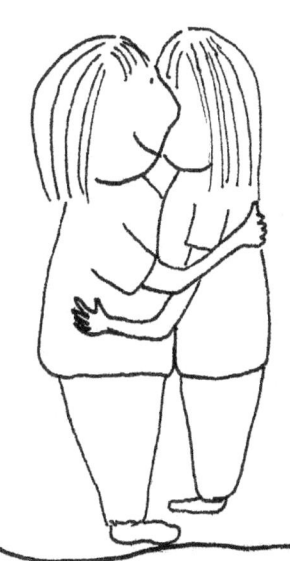

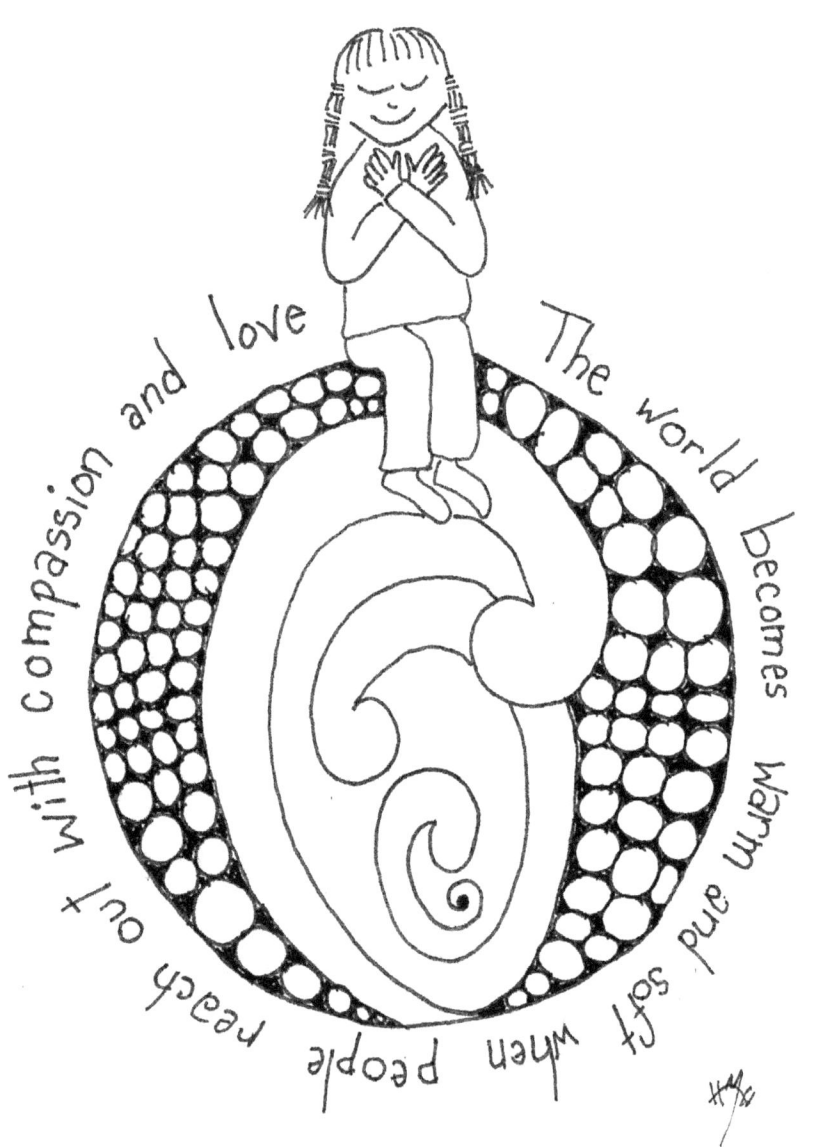

Today I recommit to being the change I wish to see in the world.
I spread love & compassion wherever I go.
I create soft, warm places.

Today may I break through the clouds and add sunshine to someone's day. May I be the help that transforms their impossible to possible.

Dream

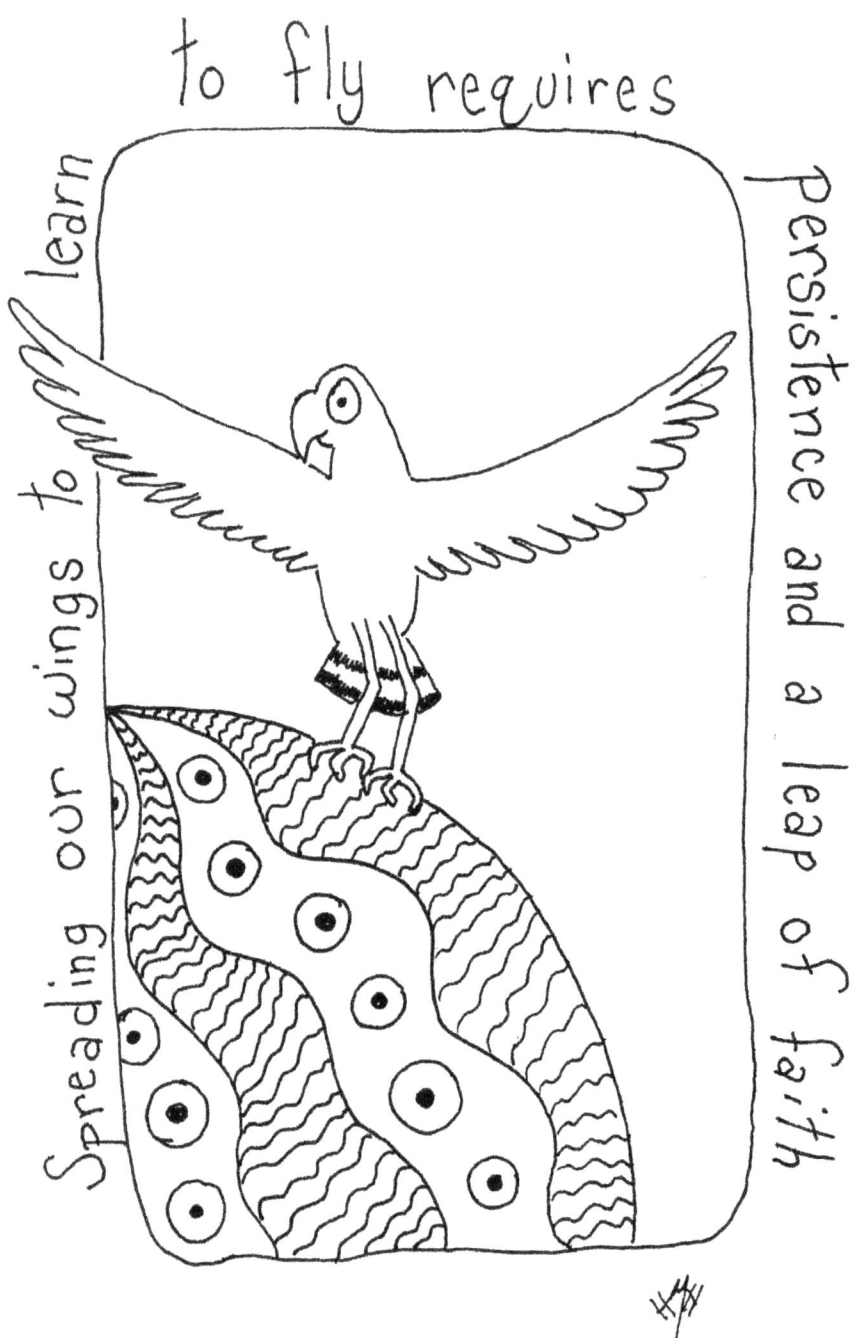

Today I will keep trying new possibilities, repeating my experiments, and perfecting my techniques. Eventually, I <u>WILL</u> prevail!

Today I see what is not there. My imagination blossoms. Dreams are born.

Today I show up.
Ideas manifest and grow.
Little things
become big things
one breath, one choice,
one step at a time.
Dreams come true.

About the Author/Illustrator

Heather Hawk Maxwell uses massage therapy, art and writing to help people create joy-filled lives, thrive through life's storms, and grow their dreams. Heather enjoys meditation, qi gong, birding and sunny days. She lives in Madison, Wisconsin with her wife, daughters and three dogs. Visit her at CreateThriveGrow.com.

www.ingramcontent.com/pod-product-compliance
Lightning Source LLC
Chambersburg PA
CBHW071120090426
42736CB00012B/1965